See the USA

CHICAGO
ILLINOIS

by
Mary Turck

CRESTWOOD HOUSE

New York

LIBRARY OF CONGRESS CATALOGING IN PUBLICATION DATA

Turck, Mary
   Chicago, Illinois / by Mary Turck : edited by Marion Dane Bauer.

   p. cm. — (See the U.S.A.)
   Includes index.
   SUMMARY: Highlights the attractions of the "Windy City," discussing its history and people as well.
   1. Chicago (Ill.)—Description—1981—Guidebooks—Juvenile literature. [1. Chicago (Ill.)—Description—Guides.] I. Bauer, Marion Dane. II. Title. III. Series.
F548.18.T87   1989   917.73'110443—dc20   89-7724
ISBN 0-89686-469-3   CIP
                                                              AC

PHOTO CREDITS

Cover: Illinois Department of Commerce and Community Affairs
Ned Skubic: 4, 7, 15, 16, 17, 19, 21, 42
Chicago Convention and Visitors Bureau: 9, 11, 20, 23, 29, 34, 37, 41
Frank Sloan: 13, 27
Illinois Department of Commerce and Community Affairs: (Terry Farmer) 18, 25, 31, 36, 39

Edited by Marion Dane Bauer

Copyright © 1989 by Crestwood House, Macmillan Publishing Company

Macmillan Publishing Company
866 Third Avenue
New York, NY 10022
Collier Macmillan Canada, Inc.

CRESTWOOD HOUSE

Produced by Carnival Enterprises

Printed in the United States of America

First Edition

10 9 8 7 6 5 4 3 2 1

CONTENTS

Introducing Chicago

Chicago is called the "Windy City." The wind whips up white-caps along **Lake Michigan.** In the summer, a constant parade of swimmers and sunbathers fills the beaches. In the winter, only a few people walk along the icy shore, but even then the frozen lakefront has an icy beauty.

The wind whistles down the canyons of **LaSalle Street.** These canyon walls are formed by tall office buildings, not by rocks. LaSalle Street's canyons are home to lawyers and stockbrokers, rather than foxes and lizards. Chicago's nickname really comes from them, too. A newspaper editor first called Chicago the "Windy City" in 1890. He meant that people there made larger-than-life boasts about their city.

The poet **Carl Sandburg** called Chicago the "City of Big Shoulders." He wrote of its bustle and vitality. Sandburg also called Chicago "Hog Butcher for the World." Years ago, this was true. Millions of cows and hogs passed through Chicago stockyards, but now the stockyards are closed.

Chicago has been the home of many famous writers. **Edgar Lee Masters,** author of *Spoon River Anthology,* lived in Chicago. The Chicago poet **Gwendolyn Brooks** wrote about the black, or African-American, experience there. She won a Pulitzer Prize.

During the 1920s and 1930s, Chicago was a wide-open town. Gangsters like **Al Capone** had more power than the mayor or chief of police. Capone terrorized much of Chicago. He rode around the city's streets in a seven-ton, bullet-proof car. Other Chicago gangsters had colorful names like "Hinky Dink" Kenna, "The Bath" Coughlin, and George "Bugs" Moran.

Sam "Momo" Giancana came to power a few decades after Al Capone. When he was young, he worked for "The Waiter" and "Big Tuna." In later years, he ran the mob in Chicago. In 1975 he was shot to death in his basement. Police are sure his assassin was part of the mob, but the killer has never been found.

Jane Addams was a different kind of famous Chicagoan. She was an organizer who cared about the poor. Her work ranged from improving garbage collection to producing plays. She

A breathtaking view of Chicago from the Sears Tower

founded **Hull House** in 1889. Hull House was a settlement house. It helped poor people by providing services like day care, a music school, and a gymnasium. Hull House is now open as a museum. Jane Addams also worked for women's rights and won the Nobel Peace Prize in 1931.

Hard-working people have come to Chicago from every country of the world. They have labored in Chicago's factories and businesses. Because they were treated badly by their employers, they formed unions. Unions were organized to protect working people.

Chicago's people include laborers and social workers, poets, gangsters, and politicians. They come from every continent and country of the world. Their colorful pasts and variety-filled present will unfold for you in Chicago.

Arriving in Chicago

If you fly into Chicago, you will land at **O'Hare** or **Midway** airports. Midway seems tiny in contrast to O'Hare, which is the world's busiest airport. More than 50 million people pass through O'Hare every year. If you fly into O'Hare, be sure to try out the "people-movers." These moving sidewalks make getting around the huge airport a little easier.

Chicago's many expressways are as busy as O'Hare Airport. The jumble of expressways includes Interstate Highways 90 and 94, 80 and 55, 57, and 290, and more. Chicago expressways have names as well as numbers—the Dan Ryan, the Kennedy, the Stevenson, the Congress, the Eisenhower, and the Edens are among them.

Trains and buses also bring people to Chicago. Chicago's railroads are the center of all United States train traffic. **Union Station** and **Northwestern Station** are huge caverns busy with crowds. Many of the passengers are commuters going to work or school, but some travel across the country.

The Illinois Central is an electric train, and its main station is located underground at the corner of Randolph and Michigan avenues. You can ride it south to the **Museum of Science and In-**

The many on and off ramps of Chicago's expressways

dustry. One special attraction at the **Illinois Central Station** is the juice bar at the entrance, which offers dozens of exotic fruit and vegetable juice combinations. Sometimes street musicians play in and near the entrance to the station, too.

The **Greyhound Bus Station** is in the center of downtown Chicago. On any day, you can see a wide variety of people there. On one side, a tired mother sits with a baby. She is waiting in the special "women and children only" section. On the other side, a man is drinking from a bottle in a paper bag. Dirt from a thousand people's shoes is ground into the floor. Police walk through, looking for runaway children or drug dealers. The Greyhound station is not a place to visit alone! But the city plans to build a new, cleaner bus station in a few years.

Chicago's Beginnings

Chicago's name comes from a Native American word that might be "she-kag-ong" or "Che-cau-go." The word means something like "wild onion" or "garlic" place. Some people say it means "skunk cabbage." Others believe it just means "a big stink."

No one is quite sure which Native American people gave Chicago its name, so no one is quite sure which word is right. There were many Native Americans living in the Chicago area before the city was built. Illinois, Miamis, Weas, and Pottawatomies were some of the tribes.

Chicago is in the state of Illinois. The state takes its name from the Illinois Native Americans.

The first Europeans to come to Illinois were fur traders. Many of them were French. Like other Europeans, they did not consider the rights of the Native American people. Although the Native Americans were living there first, the French claimed the land. They wanted it for part of New France.

In 1763, the French made a treaty with the English, giving this part of New France to the English. Then the colonists rebelled against England. They formed a new country—the United States. Illinois became part of its Northwest Territory.

Many more white settlers soon came to Illinois. The Native Americans fought back. They wanted to defend their homes and land. After all, they had been here first! But the United States sent armies against these people. By 1833 the last Native Americans were driven away. They were forced to give up their lands to the white settlers.

The first non-Native American settler of Chicago was not white. He was an African-American man named **Jean Baptiste Point du Sable.** He built a house about 1780. That was the beginning of Chicago.

Some people say Jean du Sable's father was French. Others say he was a runaway slave. Still others say he came from Santo Domingo. Wherever he came from, du Sable did well in Chicago. In 1800, he sold his trading post and home to a French trader. His property included a house, mill, bakehouse, dairy, smokehouse, poultry house, workshops, stable, and barn!

Jean Baptiste Point du Sable married a Native American woman. She was from the Pottawatomie people. They had three children in Chicago. After 1800, they moved to Missouri, where Jean du Sable died in 1813.

From Trading Post to City

Chicago was officially organized as a village in 1831. About 200 people lived in the new town.

Those were rough and ready days, and the new town grew fast. By 1835, the population was more than 2,000. By 1840, it had reached 4,470, and swarms of immigrants kept coming.

Chicago's streets were muddy when it rained in the spring and fall and dusty in the summer. Board sidewalks were laid to make

Chicago has risen from swampy marshes to dusty roads to expressways and skyscrapers.

walking easier. An early law said traffic on bridges could go no faster than a walk. Still people kept coming to Chicago. And the city kept growing. By 1858, 93,000 people lived there.

Illinois was a border state that lay between the "slave states" of the South and the "free states" of the North. Illinois almost made slavery legal in 1824, but by the 1850s many people strongly opposed slavery. People who wanted to end slavery were called "abolitionists." They wanted to abolish slavery.

One Illinois abolitionist was **the Reverend Elijah Lovejoy.** He published an anti-slavery newspaper in Illinois that ran stories about ending slavery. Angry pro-slavery mobs wrecked his presses. But he continued to fight against slavery until 1837, when Lovejoy's enemies killed him.

In 1842, a jealous white worker accused a black co-worker named **Edwin Heathcock** of being a runaway slave. So the police arrested Mr. Heathcock. He was held in jail for six weeks and was to be sold at an auction. The abolitionists organized. They got a large crowd to come to the auction and remain silent. The sheriff was frustrated because no one would bid. Finally, a judge named Ogden bid twenty-five cents. Since there was no other bid, Ogden's bid was accepted. Judge Ogden then set Mr. Heathcock free.

Runaway slaves often made their way to Chicago. If arrested, they could be sold, but many Chicagoans helped the runaways escape. Once they reached Canada, they were safe and free. This system of helping slaves was called the Underground Railroad. Each house where a runaway could stay was a "railroad station." Each person who helped was a "conductor."

In 1860, the Republicans came to Chicago to hold their National Convention. There they chose **Abraham Lincoln**, who was raised in Illinois, to run for president. After a close race, he won the election.

Lincoln became president on March 4, 1861, and on April 12, the Civil War began. Chicago sent many soldiers to fight in the war. During the war, Lincoln signed the Emancipation Proclamation. After the war, every slave in the United States was set free.

The Great Chicago Fire

Throughout the 1800s, Chicago kept on growing. By 1871, the city was home to 300,000 people and was made up of 60,000 buildings.

Over half of these buildings were made of wood. Chicago's sidewalks and pavements were also made of wood. The city was growing fast and there was no time to build solid, fireproof buildings. Chicago needed to be settled quickly, people said. They would build better houses and factories later.

The summer of 1871 was hot and dry. Small fires broke out in parts of the city, but were soon put out. Some people worried about a huge fire. But most Chicagoans had faith in the newly built **Chicago Water Tower.** They thought the water tower could pump enough water from Lake Michigan to put out any fire.

The Chicago Water Tower was completed in the mid-1800s and was one of the few buildings that survived the Great Chicago Fire.

Early on Sunday, October 8, a fire was reported on the west side of the city. By the time the firefighters arrived, three barns, a paint shop, and a shed were on fire. One popular story blames the start of the fire on Mrs. O'Leary's cow. The story says the cow kicked over a lantern. This is probably not the way the fire started, but no one knows for sure.

Firefighters could not keep the blaze under control. The fire spread swiftly northward. By 10 A.M. firefighters were battling three separate fires. Chicagoans began to panic. They ran from the flames with all the possessions they could carry. Some people buried their silver and china so they would not be destroyed by the flames. Some even buried their pianos, hoping to dig them up after the fire was put out.

The roar of the flames and the crash of falling walls could be heard everywhere. From a distance the city glowed yellow and red.

By Tuesday the fires were under control. People began to look at the damage. Over 2,000 acres in the center of the city were burned. Three hundred people were known dead; 90,000 were homeless. Trains carrying food and clothing arrived from New York and other cities. Storekeepers who had lost their buildings set up their businesses in their homes. The city had suffered a terrible loss, but rebuilding began immediately.

Many of the best architects came to Chicago to help rebuild the city. By 1885, Chicago became famous for its beautifully designed buildings. Chicago was a lively, hard-working town once again.

Unions and Strikes

In the 1800s, working conditions were not good, and workers had little power. If a boss said to work 14 hours, a worker couldn't argue. He would be fired! If a worker complained about unsafe conditions, he would be fired for that, too.

So workers organized unions. If all the workers spoke together, the boss would be more likely to listen. Early unions demanded an eight-hour day. In February 1886, the workers at the McCormick reaper factory in Chicago went on strike.

The Wrigley Building (left) and Tribune Tower (right) are two examples of Chicago's striking architecture.

On May 3, 1886, several workers were killed by the police at the McCormick plant. Workers rallied at **Haymarket Square** the next day to protest the killings. Someone threw a bomb. Then the police tried to break up the rally and fighting began.

By the time the fighting was over, seven police officers were dead. No one claimed to be responsible. Eight people were convicted of conspiracy, even though none of them was directly connected to the bomb. But since they organized the rally, they were found guilty. Four of them were hanged, and one committed suicide.

Many people said their conviction was unjust. In 1893, Governor **John Altgeld** pardoned those who were still alive.

By 1927, the average worker in Chicago still made only $15.43 a week. Union organizers continued to work for better conditions. Today Chicago has some of the country's strongest unions.

Sears Tower and John Hancock

The two tallest buildings in Chicago are the **Sears Tower** and the **John Hancock Building.**

The John Hancock Building was built in the late 1960s. Chicagoans were very proud of it because it was the tallest building in the world.

Then New York built the World Trade Center, which is taller than the John Hancock Building. So Chicago was in second place again—but not for long.

The Sears Tower was built in 1973. It is 110 stories tall and rises 1,454 feet above the ground. Chicago had the world's tallest building once again.

You can visit both the John Hancock Building and the Sears Tower. They both have observation decks near the top, and from their heights you can see all of Chicago and beyond. On a clear day you can see Wisconsin and Indiana as well as Lake Michigan.

The Sears Tower has 103 elevators. Twenty-five thousand people go in and out of it every day. If you spread out all of its space on the ground, the Sears Tower would cover 16 city blocks.

The 110-story Sears Tower

North of the Loop, visitors can hire a horse and buggy for a peaceful ride through Chicago.

Because it is so tall, the Sears Tower needs special fire rules. It has sprinkler systems and smoke detectors all over. It even has special fire-resistant wastebaskets. If a match or lighted cigarette is dropped in a wastebasket, the basket collapses, putting out the fire.

The Sears Tower is located on the southwest corner of the **Loop.** The Loop is the name of Chicago's downtown area. It is called the Loop because elevated trains run in a loop around the heart of downtown Chicago.

The John Hancock Building is on North Michigan Avenue, north of the Loop. This area is also called the **Magnificent Mile.**

North Michigan Avenue has very expensive shops. You can look in shop windows at furs and gold, and enjoy the area whether you buy something or not. Next to the John Hancock Building is **Water Tower Place,** a modern shopping center with glass elevators. As you ride up and down you can see the latest fashions on display.

Water Tower Place is across the street from the Chicago Water Tower. This is a small stone building with a visitor center. It is one of the few buildings that survived the Great Chicago Fire.

New skyscrapers dwarf the Water Tower.

Parasailers try their luck in chilly Lake Michigan.

Geography and Climate

Located on Lake Michigan, Chicago has high humidity. The average low temperature in the wintertime is 18 to 20 degrees above zero. But the humidity makes it seem colder.

Average high temperatures in the summer are only about 82 degrees, but high humidity makes summers seem hotter. At night cool breezes from the lake usually break the heat. Long ago, people slept outside in parks in the summer heat. Now the only people sleeping in parks are homeless.

Winter in Chicago brings snow, but there are frequent thaws. Chicago rarely has large amounts of snow. But the winter of 1978-79 was an exception. So much snow fell that winter that the streets could not be cleared.

The city is located on the **Chicago River.** In its early years, much of Chicago was deep in mud and marsh, but the wet land was drained into the river and canals. The Chicago River is an important link for river navigation. The river is also a marvel of engineering: Its flow was turned backward for the convenience of the city!

Boat rides on the river and Lake Michigan run through the spring, summer, and fall. The longest rides are two hours and show you most of the lakefront and downtown. The shortest rides are seven minutes—these are for commuters! Yes, in Chicago, some people ride boats to work!

Lake Michigan runs along the entire east side of Chicago. Lake Michigan is one of the Great Lakes. Its beaches offer a parade of swimsuit fashions in warm weather, while in winter ice floes crash along the shore. The lake also affects Chicago weather. Because of the lake, the temperature can drop 20 or 30 degrees in a single day.

The Chicago River flows through the middle of downtown Chicago.

The glass and steel State of Illinois Building

Chicago Seasons

Summer in Chicago brings sunny days and music. Summer is the perfect time to stroll through downtown. Outdoor art is all over Chicago's downtown.

Start your summer walking tour at Clark and Randolph. A giant glass and steel building covers a whole block. This is the **State of Illinois Building.**

Across the street is a tall, rusty-looking building. This is another government building, the **Daley Center.** It is named after the most famous and most powerful mayor in Chicago's history— **Richard Daley.** The building, though, is not really rusty. The Daley Center was built with a special kind of steel called cor-ten that is supposed to look that way!

The Picasso Statue stands in Daley Plaza.

20

In front of the Daley Center is a large plaza with a fountain and an eternal flame. The eternal flame is in honor of the late President **John F. Kennedy.** Kennedy's election was very close, and people sat up late listening to the radio and watching television to find out who won. Mayor Richard Daley's control of Chicago's votes helped Kennedy win the election.

Daley Plaza is also home to a Chicago landmark—the **Picasso Statue. Pablo Picasso** created this 50-foot-high sculpture, which is made of steel and weighs 135 tons. At first, many Chicagoans didn't like the sculpture. They were not sure what it was. Could it be a bird? A plane? A woman? An Afghan hound? No one knew for sure, but after a while, most Chicagoans decided that they liked it anyway.

Several other statues decorate outdoor Chicago. One, by **Joan Miró,** is called "Chicago." It's just across Washington Avenue and looks like a woman holding a pitchfork. Another is an 85-foot ceramic mosaic a few blocks away in front of the First National Bank Building. It shows the four seasons and was created by **Marc Chagall.**

The Federal Building hosts a red steel bird, an **Alexander Calder** creation called "Flamingo." Calder also created a motorized mobile in the lobby of the Sears Tower. This mobile is called "Universe."

Autumn in Chicago is beautiful, too. The parks and forest preserves are bright with changing colors. Chicago has lots of parades, with each of its ethnic groups claiming a special day. On Columbus Day in October the Italian community celebrates with a giant parade downtown.

November brings Thanksgiving. A visit to **Marshall Field's** on the day after Thanksgiving is a Chicago tradition. There are many Marshall Field's stores in the Chicago area, but the downtown store is special. Every Christmas the windows are filled with elab-

Alexander Calder's "Flamingo" stands in front of the Federal Building.

orate displays. One window might feature a family of bears dressed for Christmas. Another window might have a ski slope. Tiny figures move up and down the hills all day long.

January or February brings the Chinese New Year with special celebrations in **Chinatown.** A wonderful dragon leads the Chinese New Year parade. After the Chinese New Year, as the city shivers in the winter chill, most activities move indoors. But only until March. By then spring is in the air and the first celebration of spring comes from the Irish.

Chicago has a very large Irish community. And on St. Patrick's Day, they say that everyone is Irish! The St. Patrick's Day parade is Chicago's biggest spring show. The Chicago River is dyed green, many bars color beer green for the day, and a green stripe is painted down the middle of State Street.

After St. Patrick's Day, summer doesn't feel far away. Soon it will be time again for beaches, picnics, and roller-skating in **Lincoln Park,** and perhaps another walking tour.

People in Chicago

Chicago Sports

Chicago boasts two baseball teams. On the north side, the National League team, the Chicago Cubs, plays at **Wrigley Field.** Until 1988, Wrigley Field had no lights. Many people thought that was good, because they wanted baseball to be a daytime game. But now there are lights, and the Cubs can play at night, too.

The American League team, the Chicago White Sox, plays on the south side in **Comiskey Park.** Chicago fans are loyal either to the Sox or the Cubs. Often they pick the team on their own side of town.

Chicagoans dream about the day when the two teams will win both pennants. Then they could have an all-Chicago World Series! The last time that happened was 1906 when the Cubs won.

Basketball is also a popular game in Chicago. The Chicago Bulls

Baseball fans can enjoy their favorite sport in either Wrigley Field or Comiskey Park.

play at **Chicago Stadium** and Chicago has many fine college basketball teams, too. The DePaul Blue Demons have been ranked first in the country.

The Chicago Bears play football at **Soldier Field** with Chicago football fans united behind them. Chicago has a soccer team, too—the Chicago Sting.

Chicago also has a hockey team—the Chicago Black Hawks. The Black Hawks are often a winning team. Maybe that is because of the nature of hockey, which one sportswriter described as "an alley fight on skates." Chicago is a tough town. Alley fighting comes naturally!

Chicago's Neighborhoods

Chicago is a city of neighborhoods. One book lists 77 different neighborhoods, and there may actually be even more. Each neighborhood has its own name. People who live in each neighborhood find reasons to be proud of it.

Many different ethnic groups live in Chicago. Blacks, Puerto Ricans, Swedes, Mexicans, Poles, Italians, Greeks, Germans—the list goes on and on.

You can visit an old Italian neighborhood near Western and Cermak. This neighborhood is called **Little Tuscany.** Small homes and apartment buildings crowd the narrow streets.

Halsted Street near Monroe boasts a collection of Greek restaurants and shops. At night the restaurants can be exciting. Many people order an appetizer called saganaki that is set on fire before it is served. As the waiter puts out the fire with juice from a lemon, he shouts "Opaa!" This area was once home to Chicago's Greek community. Now most Greek people live on the northwest side.

The north side has many ethnic communities, too. **Andersonville** is a Swedish community. Nearby **Edgewater** has many Southeast Asian immigrants.

On the north and northwest sides, old German neighborhoods are next to old Polish neighborhoods. The south and west sides of the city are where the Irish used to live. Today, many Irish live in **Bridgeport** to the south, but there are no signs to tell which nationality lives where. Many of the neighborhoods are quite mixed.

Chinatown is located on the south side, around Cermak and Wentworth. Street signs in Chinese and English welcome visitors. Many shops offer Chinese imports. This is a good place to shop for souvenirs. Some of the restaurants offer "dim sum." This is a buffet of unusual and inexpensive foods. Some examples are spring rolls, chicken feet, and dumplings!

Blacks in Chicago

Many black people came to Chicago in the 1940s. They left the South to find jobs, hoping for a better life in Chicago. They found a city deeply divided by racism.

Racism did not arrive with the immigrants. It had been part of

In the summer, Grant Park hosts the popular food fair The Taste of Chicago.

Chicago life for decades. In 1919, whites stoned and drowned a young black man at a swimming beach. This sparked riots, with white men pursuing and killing blacks. The riots did not stop until troops were called in.

In spite of this racism, black people built strong communities. Large numbers of black people live on the south side.

Some of the neighborhoods here are **Woodlawn, Oakland, Kenwood,** and **Hyde Park.** Another large African-American community is on the west side. This community is known as **Lawndale.** African-Americans owned the churches, homes, and businesses in their communities. But since 1960, gangs and drugs have become major problems, weakening the communities.

"Urban renewal" brought more problems. Sometimes buildings were torn down, and new housing was not built. Sometimes the government built public housing projects. The public housing projects were tall, crowded apartment buildings with low rents.

Cabrini Green is one of the largest housing projects. It is a neighborhood on the north side. More than 99 percent of the people who live there are black. Cabrini Green is made up of a housing project with many tall, crowded apartment buildings and a few row houses. Since the government built the housing project for poor people, all of the people in Cabrini Green are also poor.

In the 1960s, **Dr. Martin Luther King, Jr.** came to Chicago. At that time Chicago neighborhoods were strictly segregated. Blacks were not allowed to buy houses in white areas. Dr. King wanted to integrate Chicago neighborhoods. He led marches in white neighborhoods. The marchers were stoned by angry white people.

Today blacks are the largest ethnic group in Chicago. In 1983, **Harold Washington** became Chicago's first black mayor. His election was a sign of progress. He held office until he died in 1987.

Progress has not ended all problems, however. Divisions between blacks and whites are still alive in Chicago. Traditional black and white neighborhoods have been weakened and many successful people have moved to the suburbs.

Latinos in Chicago

Spanish is Chicago's second language. People from many Spanish-speaking places have come here to live. They come from Puerto Rico, Cuba, Mexico, Spain, and countries in Central and South America. They have many different backgrounds, customs, and cultures. What they have in common is the Spanish language.

A large Mexican community lives between 18th and 26th streets. **Pilsen** and **"Little Village"** are two of the Mexican neighborhoods on Chicago's south side.

Cuban immigrants often settle on the north side. Other Latino residents come from El Salvador, Guatemala, Argentina, and other countries.

Most immigrants come to this country looking for a better life.

28

Sometimes they are looking for freedom. Sometimes they are looking for jobs. In the last century, many immigrants came from Europe. In the late 20th century, many have come from Latin America and Asia.

Parks and Zoos

Some of Chicago's parks stretch for miles along Lake Michigan's shore. Other parks are in the heart of the city. County forest preserves on the edges of the city have walking and biking trails that go for miles.

Grant Park

Grant Park is located between Lake Michigan and the Loop. Grant Park has beautiful gardens in the summer. At night its main attraction is spectacular **Buckingham Fountain**, where changing colors light up the rising and falling water.

During the warmer months, bright lights shine on Grant Park's Buckingham Fountain.

Both Grant Park and Lincoln Park were exciting places in 1968. That was the year of the Democratic Convention in Chicago during the time of the Vietnam War.

Many people wanted the war to end. They came from all over the country to protest the war. On the first night many camped in Lincoln Park until Chicago police came and drove them out.

Today Grant Park is peaceful and the streets around it are full of traffic. But in 1968 there were army tanks on the streets. People ran from the police while Red Cross medics tried to help the wounded. Police attacked reporters, too.

Joined by convention delegates, the demonstrators also conducted a candlelight march.

Now you will probably not see protesters. But if you are in Grant Park in mid-summer, you could see hot dogs and hoagies, pizza and giros at the annual Taste of Chicago. For several days, visitors sample foods from many different Chicago restaurants. Live entertainment and delicious odors make this food fair extra special. During the rest of the summer, concerts are held in the Grant Park bandshell. The Fourth of July concert comes complete with fireworks.

Lincoln Park

Lincoln Park is on the lake shore on the north side. In the summer you can rent roller skates for the day and zoom up and down the sidewalks. You can tour the park on skates, but there is a lot to see off the sidewalks, too.

Lincoln Park has many flower gardens and an indoor conservatory. Winter is an especially good time to visit the giant indoor gardens of the conservatory. Even when it is snowing outside, inside the flowers bloom!

Or you can sit on a bench and watch the people. Joggers in all sizes and shapes puff past. Near Fullerton Avenue, people play chess on outdoor tables. Groups of schoolchildren arrive with their teachers. You might want to follow them into the zoo.

Lincoln Park Zoo

Lincoln Park Zoo is free, and it is wonderful! Lincoln Park Zoo has about 2,500 animals. You can see them all quite easily as Lincoln Park Zoo covers only 35 acres.

Be sure to see the Great Ape House. Chimpanzees, orangutans, and other apes live here in a giant, glass-walled dome. They have trees to climb and ropes to swing on. You walk in a circle around their living area, looking at them through the glass.

Once an ape escaped. He found a way to get out through the roof. He ran wild through the zoo until he finally was captured. The next day thousands of people came to the zoo, setting an attendance record. They wanted to see the ape escape again.

Lincoln Park Zoo also has very friendly giraffes. They stay indoors in the winter, as do many other animals.

Curious giraffes and many other animals are at home in Lincoln Park and Brookfield zoos.

Of course, polar bears love winter. They swim and play in a large pool. You can watch them through an underwater glass window.

Feeding the seals is also fun. You can buy fish and throw it to the seals, or you can just watch as they jump and beg for the fish other people feed them.

Another part of the zoo features a Farm-in-the-Zoo with farm animals like cows, sheep, and horses.

Nearby is a special nursery for baby animals. You might see a furry little leopard, or a zookeeper giving a bottle to a baby monkey. This nursery also has a petting zoo, where visitors can reach out and touch small, furry animals!

Brookfield Zoo

Brookfield Zoo is larger than Lincoln Park Zoo. Brookfield Zoo has about 2,000 animals (500 less than Lincoln Park has). But it covers 200 acres. That is nearly six times as much land as Lincoln Park Zoo, so you can do a lot of walking. Or you can ride on the safari trains that take people around Brookfield.

Each season brings different activities to Brookfield Zoo. During the summer the Children's Zoo has "Animals in Action" programs and a Teddy Bear Picnic. In December you will find the Holiday Magic Festival.

It also has Tropic World, the largest indoor exhibit in the world. Birds, gorillas, and monkeys roam free. Hundreds of other animals share the rain forests. The Tropic World has three rain forests modeled after the rain forests of Africa, Asia, and South America.

The Seven Seas exhibit has sea lions, seals, and a walrus. Dolphins perform in the "Dolphinarium." There are seats for 2,000 visitors here!

Brookfield Zoo is open every day. Usually there is an admission fee, but on Tuesdays it is free. Brookfield is about 14 miles west of downtown Chicago. You can reach the zoo by train, bus, or car.

Great Museums

Chicago has dozens of fine museums. Some are very specialized, such as the **Peace Museum,** the **Printers Row Printing Museum,** the **International Museum of Surgical Sciences,** or the **American Police Museum.** Others offer something for almost everyone. And a few were made especially for children.

Museum of Science and Industry

The Museum of Science and Industry is huge. It has about 2,000 exhibits. Many of them are "hands-on," which means you can actually run them.

The Space Center focuses on outer space. The Apollo 8 spacecraft is there. The Omnimax theater shows films every hour.

Another popular exhibit is a 16-foot model of a human heart. You can walk right through it!

At Christmas time, there are trees from around the world. Each tree is decorated as it would be in foreign countries such as Korea, Japan, England, or Denmark.

Would you like to see the Fairy Castle? Or do you prefer a full-size, captured German U-boat? How about a trip through a coal mine? You can tour all of these at the Museum of Science and Industry. Admire the Fairy Castle. Walk through the submarine. Travel deep underground in the coal mine. The Museum of Science and Industry has something for everyone. And it is all free!

Field Museum

The **Field Museum of Natural History** is also on the lake shore. It is one of the greatest natural history museums in the world.

Dioramas are a special part of the Field Museum. Dioramas are life-size exhibits of animals in their natural settings. The animals in the exhibits are stuffed—not live—but they look right at home. One diorama of an African water hole has 23 animals.

The Hall of Dinosaurs has giant skeletons. You can see life on Earth from prehistoric times to the present! Some exhibits let you use microscopes. Others let you touch and feel the artifacts. (Artifacts are the things on exhibit—like stone knives or animal skins.)

You could spend days exploring the Field Museum and its nine acres of exhibits. The great variety of exhibits means there is something interesting for everyone. The museum has just about everything from ancient Egyptian mummies to collections of jade and jewels. Check for special family activities, too.

Native American cultures are shown here in seven exhibit halls. The Field Museum has a special resource center for Native American cultures. The Pawnee Earth Lodge is 38 feet long. Here you can sit inside the lodge on a buffalo robe, see and touch special Pawnee artifacts, and learn how the country's first residents lived.

"A Place for Wonder" is a special part of the Field Museum. This is a hands-on room. You can touch fossils and furs, hooves and horns. Or would you like to touch a meteorite? You may try on Chinese costumes from long ago. And you can learn to use chopsticks.

The botany section has tree trunks cut in half. Its "smelly section" offers vanilla beans, cinnamon, and much more. The geology section has a dinosaur bone and a woolly mammoth tooth to touch. "A Place for Wonder" has something for everyone!

Thursday is a free day at the Field Museum. Other days there is an admission charge. It is closed on Thanksgiving, Christmas, and New Year's Day.

Shedd Aquarium

The **Shedd Aquarium** is the world's biggest indoor aquarium! It is located near the Field Museum, and you can easily walk from one to the other. Like the Field Museum, the free day for the aquarium is Thursday.

Coral reefs are re-created here in a 90,000-gallon tank. A diver feeds the fish in the tank at least twice every day and talks to visitors through a two-way microphone.

The entrance hall at the Field Museum is filled with interesting exhibits.

The main tank at the Shedd Aquarium is home to many types of fish.

Another special exhibit is one on river otters. This exhibit features a video.

More than 8,000 water animals are on display in this aquarium! Some are from fresh water. Others are from salt water. Some are mammals, some are reptiles and amphibians, and many are fish. Sea anemones are animals that look like flowers. The exhibits come from all over the world.

Seals glide underwater. Green moray eels hide in the coral reef. Bright tropical fish show off in Chinese settings. All this is found at the Shedd Aquarium.

Adler Planetarium

The **Adler Planetarium** is also near the Field Museum. You can see the building and exhibits without charge. Some exhibits show telescopes and early scientific instruments. Others show space explorations. There is even a moon rock!

You have to pay to see the Sky Shows, but they are worth it! Sky Shows begin with the multi-media Universe Theater show. Multi-media means that it uses slides, lights, sound, and pictures. These are different kinds of media. The show is on all of the walls and ceiling of the theater, so you feel as if you were out in space!

Next you move to the Sky Theater. This part of the show uses a Zeiss VI projector. The projector weighs two and one-half tons and is more than 17 feet long. The projector puts a picture of the sky and stars on a 68-foot dome.

First, it shows what the sky looks like on that night. Then it shows a special story. At Christmas, the special story is the "Star of Wonder." Another popular story is "Searching for E.T.s." There are many special stories.

The Adler Planetarium

On Saturday morning there is a special Children's Sky Show. But don't be fooled by the name! This is mostly for very little children, because children under six cannot go to the regular Sky Shows.

Chicago Historical Society

The **Chicago Historical Society** is near Lincoln Park on Clark Street and North Avenue.

Whether you enjoy history or not, this is an interesting place to visit. The Illinois Pioneer Life Gallery has daily shows with activities such as weaving, spinning, or candle dipping.

The Chicago Fire exhibit shows leaping flames and fire engines. Recorded voices tell the story, making history come alive.

Other special exhibits show old costumes and folk art. This museum has a fine display of old fashions and clothing. A listening booth has early radio broadcasts.

Besides Chicago history, there are American history exhibits. One exhibit called "We the People" tells about the birth of the United States.

The free day at this museum is Monday. It is closed on Thanksgiving, Christmas, and New Year's Day.

Express-Ways Children's Museum

Another Chicago museum especially for children is **Express-Ways Children's Museum.** It has hands-on exhibits for children from 2 to 12 years old. Two exhibits are especially good for older children. One is called Magic and Masquerade. This exhibit focuses on West Africa. You can sit in a traditional tribal home, try on costumes, and play musical instruments. It is an exciting way to learn about another part of the world.

Another exhibit is about architecture. This exhibit has five small buildings that are models of famous Chicago buildings. You can walk through the building models and see how the buildings were constructed. The buildings are the Art Institute, Cook County Hospital, the Post Office, Sears Tower, and the Chicago Tribune Building. After you have looked at the small-scale models, you might want to visit the actual buildings.

The museum's Recycle Center has lots of strange stuff. Different industries contribute their "left-overs." You can choose whatever you like for art projects. If you are planning a project, you can fill up a bag with whatever you need—and it's free!

The Express-Ways Children's Museum is planning more exhibits, so you might find even more good things when you visit.

The Art Institute

The **Art Institute** is famous all over the world. Art lovers can spend weeks seeing paintings and sculptures. For younger people, the Art Institute has a special Junior Museum with games and special exhibits.

Huge lions guard the entrance to the Art Institute.

Besides the Junior Museum, there are often special children's programs. You can call ahead to find out about these programs. Plan on visiting the Junior Museum and going to a special program. There is a lot that you might enjoy in the main part of the museum, too.

You might want to look at the arms and armor. Or you might want to see some of the most famous paintings. One of these is Grant Wood's *American Gothic.* Another is *The Assumption of the Virgin* by El Greco.

The free day at the Art Institute is Tuesday. The Art Institute is located downtown at Michigan Avenue and Adams Street. You can't miss the big stone lions standing guard at the front of the building.

Getting Around Town

Chicago has good public transportation with buses and trains to take you all over town. In some cities they stop at midnight but not here! "Owl service" continues all night long.

One way to see a lot of the city in a hurry is by the **El.** The El is an elevated train that sometimes goes underground. Then it is usually called the subway.

Sometimes there is an easier way to see museums. On Sundays, the CTA Culture Bus leaves from the Art Institute and takes you to museums on the north or south side of the city.

If your family is driving, be sure to see **Lake Shore Drive.** There is a thrilling view of the Chicago skyline from Lake Shore Drive. As you drive north toward the Loop, all of Chicago seems to sparkle in front of you.

Eating Out

Chicago claims to have the best pizza in the world. "Stuffed pizza" has several layers of cheese and filling and crust, and Chicago claims to be the place where it was invented.

The El travels noisily just above Chicago's streets.

"Deep dish" pizza has a thick crust and lots of fillings. This is the original Chicago-style pizza. **Uno's Restaurant** says it invented deep dish pizza in 1943.

Chicago also claims to have the world's best hot dogs. You can get hot dogs in dozens of small places. Many have signs hanging outside that say "Vienna Beef."

Bobby's is one popular place for hot dogs. It serves hot dogs, Polish sausage, and Italian beef sandwiches topped with sweet or hot peppers.

Other hot dog places give you different choices. Would you like sauerkraut on your hot dog? How about chili? Of course, you can always get just ketchup and mustard.

Chicago has fancy restaurants with high prices, but you don't need to spend a lot to eat well. Small, cheap places can be very good. How do you find small restaurants? Ask! Chicago people are friendly. They will tell you their favorite places for tacos or egg rolls or pizza.

41

Enjoying Chicago

Planning ahead makes any trip more fun. Be sure to bring the right clothes for Chicago weather. You may need to pack an umbrella, too.

Think about how much time you want to spend at each place you see. You might want to spend all day at the Field Museum. Or you might want to see only a small part of it so you would also have time for the nearby Shedd Aquarium.

Some basic rules for visiting big cities are:

1) Don't travel alone.

2) Don't walk far at night.

3) When in doubt, ask a hotel clerk or police officer about safety in a neighborhood.

4) Watch out for pickpockets.

Chicago is an exciting city to visit. Plan ahead and enjoy your trip!

At any time of year, visitors to Chicago can expect good food and great fun.

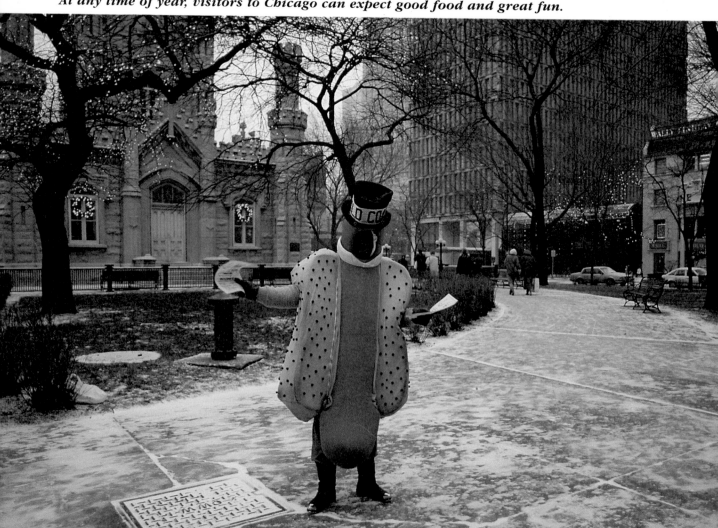

Chicago Statistics

1831:	Founded as a village
1837:	Became a city
1843:	City law passed that said pigs could not run in the streets
Chicago:	Largest city in Illinois, but not the capital (Springfield is the capital)
Number of people (as of 1989):	3 million
Chicago River:	Flows backward. The river flowed into Lake Michigan until 1900. In that year, engineers reversed the flow so sewage from the river wouldn't pollute the lake.
O'Hare Airport:	Chicago's main airport and the busiest one in the world
Tallest building:	Sears Tower (1,454 feet)
Zoos:	Brookfield Zoo Lincoln Park Zoo
Best-known museums:	Museum of Science and Industry Field Museum of Natural History Art Institute Adler Planetarium Shedd Aquarium
Other museums:	du Sable Museum of African-American History Mexican Fine Arts Center Museum
Largest park:	Lincoln Park
View from Sears Tower and John Hancock buildings:	On a clear day, visitors can see Wisconsin, Indiana, and Lake Michigan.

For More Information

For more information about Chicago, write to:

Chicago Convention of Tourism Bureau
McCormick Place on the Lake
Chicago, IL 60616

Chicago Tourism Council
Historic Water Tower in the Park
806 North Michigan Avenue
Chicago, IL 60611

Illinois Tourist Information Center
Department of Commerce and Community Affairs
310 South Michigan Avenue
Suite 108 — Ground Floor
Chicago, IL 60604

City Map

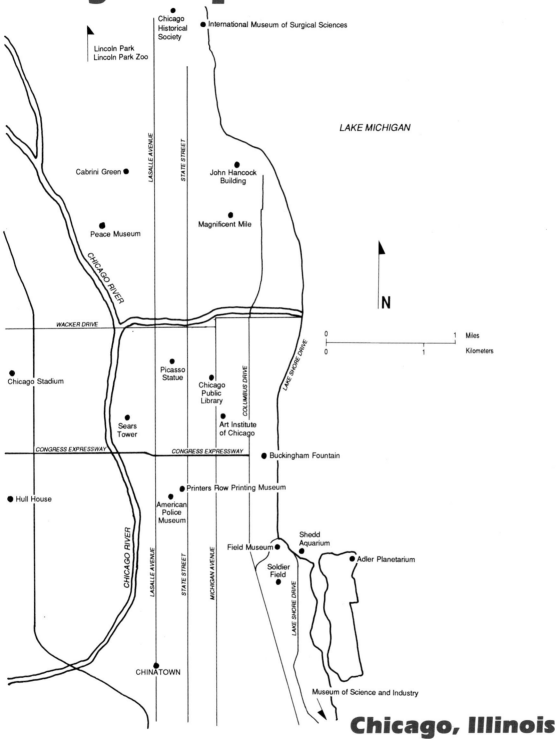

Chicago Historical Society

International Museum of Surgical Sciences

Lincoln Park
Lincoln Park Zoo

LASALLE AVENUE

STATE STREET

LAKE MICHIGAN

Cabrini Green

John Hancock Building

Peace Museum

Magnificent Mile

CHICAGO RIVER

N

WACKER DRIVE

0   1   Miles

0   1   Kilometers

Picasso Statue

Chicago Stadium

LAKE SHORE DRIVE

COLUMBUS DRIVE

Chicago Public Library

Sears Tower

Art Institute of Chicago

CONGRESS EXPRESSWAY

CONGRESS EXPRESSWAY

Buckingham Fountain

Printers Row Printing Museum

Hull House

American Police Museum

CHICAGO RIVER

LASALLE AVENUE

STATE STREET

MICHIGAN AVENUE

Shedd Aquarium

Field Museum

Adler Planetarium

Soldier Field

LAKE SHORE DRIVE

CHINATOWN

Museum of Science and Industry

Chicago, Illinois

Index
of People & Places

917.73 Turck, Mary
TU
        Chicago, Illinois

$12.95

DATE			
APR 2 8 1995			
8 7 JAN 4 2002			
CO JAN 3 1 2002			
12 JAN 1 7 2012			